GET WET!

page 2

page 12

Diana Bentley

Story illustrated by
Pet Gotohda

Heinemann

Before Reading

Find out about

- Some scary water rides

Tricky words

- water rides
- scary
- would
- dragon's mouth

Introduce these tricky words and help the reader when they come across them later!

Text starter

There are lots of different water rides. Some of the rides are very steep and in some you drop down very fast. They are very scary and you will get wet.

Water Rides

Water rides are scary
and you will get wet!

This water ride is scary.

You go fast and you get wet.

This water ride is scary.

You go into the
dragon's mouth!

Would you like to go
on this ride?

This water ride is scary.

You drop down very fast.

Would you like to go on this ride?

9

This water ride is **very** scary.

You go very fast and you get very wet!

Quiz

Text Detective

- Why do you get wet on a water ride?
- Do you like getting wet on rides?

Word Detective

- **Phonic Focus:** Final phonemes

  Page 6: Find a word that ends with the phoneme 'th'.
- Page 4: How many syllables (beats) are there in the word 'scary'?
- Page 6: Why is there an exclamation mark after 'mouth'?

Super Speller

Read these words:

get   and

Now try to spell them!

HA! HA! HA!

Q What animal never gets wet?

A An umbrellephant.

In this story

 Bones

 The master

 Wag

Tricky words

- grass
- hose
- thought
- snake
- jumped

Introduce these tricky words and help the reader when they come across them later!

Story starter

Bones is a big dog. Wag is a small dog. Bones is a very good dog but Wag is always getting into trouble. One day, their master was hanging out the washing and Bones saw a peg on the grass.

The Water Hose

Bones saw a peg on the grass.

Bones took the peg
to his master.

"Good dog, Bones,"
said his master.

Bones saw a sock on the grass.

Bones took the sock to his master.

The master gave Bones a bone.

17

Wag saw the hose
on the grass.

Wag thought the hose
was a snake.

Is it really a snake?

Wag jumped on the snake.

Wag took the snake
to his master.

"Stop! Stop!" said his master.

"Bad dog, Wag!"
said his master.

Quiz

Text Detective

- Why did the master say "Stop! Stop!"?
- Was Wag being really bad?

Word Detective

- **Phonic Focus:** Final phonemes

  Page 14: Find a word ending with the phoneme 'g'.
- Page 15: Find a smaller word inside the word 'dog'.
- Page 23: What words does the master say to Wag?

Super Speller

Read these words:

dog peg

Now try to spell them!

HA! HA! HA!

Q What is full of holes but can hold water?

A A sponge.

24